One Gorilla

ISBN-10: 1-84248-200-9
ISBN-13: 978-1-84248-200-1
This edition published 2006 by Mathew Price Limited
Albury Court, Albury
Thame, Oxfordshire OX9 2LP
Printed in China

One Gorilla

A magical kind of counting book

Atsuko Morozumi

Mathew Price Limited

Here is a list of things I love.
One gorilla.

Two butterflies among the flowers
and one gorilla.

Three budgerigars
in my house
and one gorilla.

Four squirrels in the woods
and one gorilla.

Five pandas in the snow
and one gorilla.

Six rabbits in
a field and
one gorilla.

Seven frogs by the fence
and one gorilla.

Eight fish in the sea
and one gorilla.

Nine birds among
the leaves and
one gorilla.

Ten cats in my garden
and one gorilla.

ten 10 cats

nine 9 birds

eight 8 fish

seven 7 frogs

six 6 rabbits

five 5 pandas

four 4 squirrels

three 3 budgerigars

two 2 butterflies

But where is my gorilla?

Ah, there he is.